# $\mathscr{P}$resentation $\mathscr{P}$age

A gift from _____

to _____

Date _____

Occasion _____

_____ No occasion, just because I love you

# Also by Marjabelle Young Stewart

*White Gloves and Party Manners*
(with Ann Buchwald)

*Stand Up, Shake Hands, Say "How Do You Do"*
(with Ann Buchwald)

*Executive Etiquette* (with Marian Faux)

*Your Complete Wedding Planner*

*The New Etiquette*

*Can My Bridesmaids Wear Black?*

# LITTLE WAYS
## TO SAY
## YOU CARE

---

MARJABELLE YOUNG STEWART

MJF BOOKS
NEW YORK

Published by MJF Books
Fine Communications
322 Eighth Avenue
New York, NY 10001

*Little Ways to Say You Care*
LC Control Number 2002102489
ISBN 1-56731-530-5

$\mathcal{C}$ontents

# Acknowledgments

A loving special thank you to Marian Faux, whose excellent writing skill, research, and gentle feelings have been invaluable in producing this book.

A special hug and a salute to my senior editor, Barbara Anderson, for being available at all times and for the recent elegant tea in my honor at the Palm Court of the Plaza Hotel.

My thanks to agent Dominick Abel, a true knight in shining armor, whose professionalism has been invaluable in developing my career, and to St. Martin's Press, the world's best publisher.

This book is lovingly dedicated to my precious family and friends. *Family:* husband Bill; daughter Jackie; son Bill Junior; granddaughter Erin Marjabelle; sisters Maxine Johnson and Eleanore Ostercamp; mother-in-law Elizabeth Stewart; cousins Goldie, Margaret, Ellene, Joan, Edith, Eva, and Aunt

Helene; godmother Dorothy Merrick; and matron of honor Sue Barnes. *Kind and loving friends:* Dr. Irene Caruso, Mother Mary, Jacquie, Elaine, Teresa, Margie, Cheryl, Patty, Sherri, Michelle, Patt, Tiffany, Shannon, Betsy, Winnie, Vicky, Mary, Marion, Barbara, Brenda, Dorel, Liz, Nancy, Rosemary, Katherine, Henrietta, Mildred, Shirley, Jerelyn, Joyce, Carol, Jan, Susan, Lora, Helen, Mary Jane, Amanda, Sharon, Carla, Rita, Ann, Toni, Rosie, Gail, Gay, Muffy, Martha, Arronlea, Lorraine, Margaret, Flora, Angel, Stacy, Jennie, Norma, Alice, Judy, Kathy, Darleen, Donna, Sue, Lorelei, Linda, Debby, Nadine, Bess, Pat, Joanne, Roxanne, Amy, Julie, Holly, Suzanne, Tammy, Joan, Donna, Faith, Diane, Lois, Sandy, Millie, Salle, Dorothy, Sarah, Lynn Barbara, Clara, Bonnie, Marta, Annette, Maeve, Linda, Gloria, Iris, Jalinda, Kathleen, Cynthia, Christine, Debbie, Sandra, Nick, Ferg, Nico, Willard, Lonnie, Andy, Wayne, John, Bob, Ben, Bernie, Bruce, Bryan, Art, Mack, Joe, Peter, Earl, Ray, Don, Tom, Mike, Gary, B.J., Max, Rodney, Father Jack, Father Remm, Jim, George, Chuck, Ron, Rocky, Phil, Charles, Jack, Doug, Roger, Bill, Harold, Todd, Cal, Vince, Mark, Chip, Jerry, Mark, Russ, Scottie, Steven, Stan, Dana, Jon, and Ed.

This is my little way to say to all of you, "I love you."

# A Word
## from Marjabelle

How many times has your day been enhanced by one small, unnecessary gesture that someone *chose* to make toward you? A special handwritten note from a good friend telling you to hang in there with a diet because you're looking great. A single perfect flower from your sister whom you're meeting for an all-too-rare lunch. A funny cartoon clipping sent for no reason other than to brighten your day. A gift of a couple hours' time from an old friend for a long, quiet walk when you were bereaved.

These small acts of kindness aren't earth-shattering, but they are often enormously touching, and the pleasure we get from them, as either receiver or giver, often far outweighs the size of the deed itself.

In today's fast-paced and pressured world, the small gesture unfortunately has become something of a lost art, something we don't bother with nearly often enough. We seem to have no time to offer the smallest courtesies to acquaintances and strangers, and all too often we don't bother with them for our dearest friends and family members either. In our failure to show others that we love them, we deprive not only others but also ourselves.

It is my hope that this small book will serve as a road map to guide you toward reinstating the little but loving gesture in your life and in the lives of those whom you love. Some of the suggestions are practical—such as the ideas for bringing extra comfort into the life of a beloved elderly relative—while others are frivolous and fun. A few are sensual. Some are spiritual—suggestions for ways to *think about* loving one another in addition to *doing* for one another.

Most of the special touches I am suggesting require little apart from your time and attention. By the end of the book, I hope you will have reached a new understanding of love, and will realize that it is the simple gift of time and attention—and not necessarily the grand gesture—that captures the hearts of others.

Having said this, however, you may also want to take a peek at a section of the book called "Grand Gestures," anecdotes of some very exceptional ways in which individuals have extended themselves for those they love.

But whether your gesture is large or small, don't forget the adage concerning every gift in the world: It's not the gift that counts, but the thought behind it.

*Marjabelle Young Stewart*

# Loving Our Partners

$\mathcal{M}$arriage is truly the most intimate relationship in the world. Like no other person, our partners know all our vulnerabilities, where all the tiny and large wounds and tics are, and where and how to strike out to give pain. No one else, not even one's parents, is privy to the familiarity and vulnerability that develop in a marriage or other close partnership.

But if it follows that one's partner has the power to hurt, he or she also has an even greater power to please and to give pleasure to his or her loved one.

Too often, though, in marriage, we let the little pleasures slip, as we begin to take one another for granted. It's inevitable, I suppose, that this will happen. After all, taking someone for granted is also part of the comfort of marriage. But—and this is the beautiful part—we don't have to take our partner for granted all the time.

I think we all would do well to take a refresher course every now and then in how to be a truly loving mate. I hope you'll think of this section as a refresher course in loving your life partner. And it's only a starting point. Once you begin applying some of the loving gestures I've described in the following pages, I'm sure your imagination and creativity will be sparked, and you'll come up with many, many more ideas of your own.

# A Love Quiz

Write a quiz made up of questions only you will know the answers to, and have your partner do the same. Settle into your favorite chairs with a soothing or refreshing drink and take each other's quizzes. Sharing the intimacy of the quiz will get you laughing, joking, perhaps even arguing a bit, and then, I hope, making up very romantically.

Here are some questions to get you started:

**1** ～ Name one ex-girlfriend or ex-boyfriend of your spouse.

**2** ～ What photos does your spouse carry in his or her wallet?

**3** ～ How many silver dollars does your spouse own?

**4** ～ What is your spouse's favorite color?

**5** ～ What is your spouse's most sentimental possession?

**6** ～ Name or describe one toy your spouse was especially attached to as a child.

**7** ～ Who is your spouse's favorite relative outside his or her immediate family?

**8** ～ What did your spouse collect as a child?

**9** ～ Who was your spouse's favorite teacher?

**10** ～ What was your spouse's highest rank in Boy Scouts or Girl Scouts?

Oh, all right, we'll throw in the big but trite one: What color are your spouse's eyes? But I warn you, this is the question that will start the argument.

## Out of Sight, But Not Out of Mind

Drop by your true love's office while he or she is out to lunch and leave a small present—

~ a single flower

~ a sampling of his favorite chocolate

~ a bag of her favorite jellybeans

~ a miniature windup toy

Beside the gift leave a brief love note, but be sure you put the note in an envelope marked "Confidential"!

## Tie Him Up—His Way

The next time you buy him a tie, buy the kind of tie he wants to wear—not what you want him to wear in your mental make-overs of him.

## Trips Etched in Time

This very special present takes time—at least three years, I would say, and perhaps longer—and a slightly conniving nature. When you and your partner go on vacation, take a picture of your mate, or of the two of you together, if possible. Be sure to set the picture in front of something that clearly identifies where you are.

I gathered funny pictures of my husband atop the Eiffel Tower, by the Grand Canyon, and on the observation deck of the Empire State Building—in each case clenching himself and making a funny face as if he were afraid he might fall. When the vacation pictures came back from being developed, I made sure to pull these prints and the negatives before he saw them.

When I had collected three photos, I had them framed together and presented them to him as a gift.

# Here's to You Alone

It's important that we build traditions into our lives, and sometimes they come from the most unexpected places. When my husband and I were given two uniquely distinctive champagne glasses that simply didn't fit with the other twelve we owned, I couldn't imagine when we would ever use them. On our first anniversary, I found out. My husband came home with a bottle of vintage champagne, to be shared at the end of our romantic evening—and using the glasses has become our special tradition as we toast each marvelous year of our marriage.

# A Warm Treat for the First Cold Sunday

On the first blustery autumn Sunday, slip out of bed early and make a special cold-weather breakfast for your mate, who'll awaken to the aroma of your special feast. Think about

~ warm, homemade muffins

~ waffles or pancakes

~ bacon and eggs

These treats are even more appreciated in these days when we all watch our diets and eat such foods less often than we used to.

# A Big Birthday

Plan a week of festivities when your partner is turning a corner into a new decade. Here are some ideas to get you started:

Give him or her a gift every day of the week.

Decorate some small corner of your home every day.

Examples: Fill the bathtub with balloons so he'll find it just before his morning shower. Put a small plant by her side of the bed. Put a "Happy Birthday" poster on the front door or the garage door. Hang crepe paper streamers from his closet.

Have a surprise party one night of the week but not on his actual birthday. (You've got better plans for the actual birthday night.) Planning a surprise party takes work but is well worth the effort, plus it truly will be a surprise if it's not held on the birthday proper.

Ask your partner's family and close friends several weeks in advance. Emphasize to everyone that the event is a secret and tell them how and where to meet so as not to give anything away. Book a restaurant or order food delivered to your home (provided your partner isn't around during the day; otherwise, ask a neighbor to accept the delivery). Either you or someone else should probably accompany your partner in the hour or so before the party when people are gathering so he or she doesn't change plans and show up early.

On the actual birthday, plan a very romantic dinner for two at your favorite restaurant. It will give your partner the opportunity to reflect on his or her wonderful week.

## Sharing a Surprise

When my friend Jill stumbled across the stunning, little-known rose garden in New York City's Central Park, she didn't rush to tell her husband, who loved gardens, all about it. Instead she insisted that he meet her one day after work on the street outside the park so she could show him something special. When he arrived by bus, she was waiting nearby with a half-liter of wine and some cheese and crackers. She loved watching his pleasure at her discovery.

Most of us want to share with our loved one whatever we find that is extraordinary or unique, but the occasion can be even more memorable if you turn it into an event, however minor, as Jill did.

So the next time you discover a previously unknown fountain, a quiet bench, a rookery, a picnic spot, or even a particularly scenic spot on a local road, don't tell your mate about it. Take him or her to it.

## Romance, à la Astaire

Enroll yourself and your loved one in a ballroom-dance class—and don't quit until you've learned to tango.

## A Sweet Reward

When your spouse is doing some unusual and much disliked household chore, such as defrosting the refrigerator or washing windows, show your appreciation by tucking away treats—candy or one-dollar bills—at strategic locations to spur him or her on.

## My Funny Valentine— All Year Long

Years ago, I began mailing outrageously funny cards and often risqué (well, mostly risqué) cards to my husband at work—cards unlike any I give him on our regular card-sending occasions. I never sign them. He knows, of course, that they are from me, but pretends he doesn't. He'll bring the card home, toss it my way, and ask me if I know anything about it. I deny everything.

I've been denying everything for twelve years now, and I think this adds a little spark to our marriage. And, of course, he's flattered by the razzing he gets at work whenever a card arrives.

## Silly Stuff

Buy a frivolous pin and wear it to greet your loved one. Last Halloween, I bought a windup toy bat pin that flapped its wings. With the bat's wings flapping, I greeted my husband at the door. Needless to say, I quickly presented the gift to him.

## Yes, We Have No Occasion

Don't send flowers just at the expected occasions such as Valentine's Day and her birthday. Most romantic of all is to send them for no occasion . . . just to say "I love you." And make sure the note you enclose makes this perfectly clear.

## Working Woman's Dinner à Deux

Plan a romantic dinner as a surprise for him one night—but keep it simple. Go all out on setting the table, arranging fresh flowers, and lighting candles, but don't kill yourself cooking. Instead, serve a simple favorite dish—a stew or a hearty soup—plus a green salad, and a special bottle of wine. That way, you won't be too tired to prolong the festivities.

# The Luxuries of Life

Most of us have a wish list of things that we would love to have but would not buy for ourselves. These often make perfect gifts to loved ones. Susie, an old friend, got tired of listening to her husband, Bill, search for his shoehorn every morning. He never seemed to put it in the same place, and it was small and easily overlooked. After months of searching, she bought him a large (and therefore, she hoped, unlosable) eighteenth-century brass shoehorn—the kind of thing he would never treat himself to but was delighted to receive.

In return, Bill noticed that in a lingerie catalog his wife had earmarked a lovely silk nightshirt, even though she tended to buy less expensive, practical nightshirts. On her next birthday, he bought her a tailored nightshirt in the most luxurious silk imaginable.

Most luxury-loving people who keep themselves in check for one reason or another are truly thrilled to be given something special that they wouldn't ordinarily buy. Watch carefully for clues to what your partner might enjoy.

# If I'd Known You Were Doing Something Special, I'd Have Baked a Cake

Don't save something as luscious as a cake for birthdays. Use it for any special occasion—when your partner gets a much-deserved promotion, a raise, a new job, or when a major project at home or work is completed.

Buy or bake the cake and decorate it with a message of congratulations.

## Making Stock

Make chicken soup *from scratch* the next time your partner is laid low with the flu.

## One Night of Luxury

Pamper your partner for one special night. Take him or her out to dinner. Arrange in advance for a menu without any prices. Pick up the tab for everything, and even be the one who drives home. (Or, if you're feeling really extravagant, rent a limousine to drive both of you home.)

## Hot Romance

Want to send a tingle down your partner's spine? Look her straight in the eye and tell her that you want the two of you to be alone. Then move heaven and earth to make sure you are. All couples need special time with their partners—without children and other family members—to renew their love for each other and simply to enjoy each other's company. Take whatever time you can afford—a night, a weekend, a week—to whisk your partner away for some special time alone together. Some possible escapes might be a walk on the beach or in the woods, a lunch together in the middle of the week, a drive-in movie, an overnight camp-out, a weekend cruise, or a ferry ride.

# Do It the Other Way

Volunteer to spend a day or two doing something you don't enjoy that your partner loves doing. Like most of us, you probably figured out a few years into your marriage that it's okay—and even healthy—to have some separate interests. But it's also important to appreciate the activities that each of you treasures.

If he wants to go antiquing and you never have the patience, go along cheerfully for a day or a weekend. Similarly, when she wants to go to a basketball game, surprise her—with two tickets and your cheerful company.

# Promises, Promises

Present your partner with a handwritten or, better yet, hand-drawn, book of coupons. Each one describes a special service you will deliver when presented with the coupon: "Good for one breakfast in bed," "Good for one fifteen-minute foot massage," "Good for one ride in the country." Be sure to include at least one coupon involving an offer to take over some task your partner especially dislikes: "Good for doing the laundry one Saturday morning while you sleep late," or "Good for sewing on one missing button."

## I'm Singing Our Songs

Create a tape of the songs that were popular when you first met—including, of course, "your song," and present it to your partner.

## Thinking of You

Tuck a perfume- or aftershave-scented handkerchief (barely scented, *not drenched*) into your partner's suitcase when he's leaving town on business, along with a note that says "Think of me."

## In My Thoughts

One couple I know leaves each other small love notes whenever one must go out of town on business. The partner who stays home finds a note on his pillow on the first night of his spouse's absence, and in the morning a note tucked into his underwear drawer, a note on the bathroom mirror or by his razor. If you're the one staying home, surprise the traveler by tucking a love note—or a photo of the two of you—into his or her suitcase.

# Mystery Days

Several couples we know plan three or four "mystery" days each year. One partner announces the date and plans the day. Without knowing where he or she is headed, the other partner goes along for the special jaunt—to a newly discovered restaurant, a botanical garden, a state park.

# A Fable

A man we know occasionally treats his wife to a gift certificate to her favorite magazine stand. Sounds mundane, you say? Hardly. *She's* thrilled. A true magazine junkie, she spends many happy and, may we add, guilt-free, hours buying expensive foreign fashion and shelter magazines that she ordinarily wouldn't treat herself to. The certificates, of a generous size, often stretch over several months.

The gift was accidental, at least the first time. My friend's husband had returned some camera film, only to be told that the store would give him credit but not a refund. At a loss as to how he would use the credit, he turned it over to his wife, who enjoyed it so much that he now routinely buys her a "newsstand gift certificate." Moral: In gift giving, never overlook the obvious or hesitate to give life's smallest pleasures.

## Whisking Her Away

Surprise your wife with an impromptu date. Call her and say, "Get dressed up. I'm taking you somewhere special for dinner tonight."

Choose a romantic setting, preferably candlelit, for your lovely dinner *à deux*.

## Stargazing

In these days of celebrity hype, think about another, more awe-inspiring kind of stargazing. Study up on the constellations and then go out and stargaze at the universe with your loved one.

## Heavenly Real Estate

Speaking of the stars, you can do more than stare at them. Buy your partner a star of his or her very own. You can do this by calling the Ministry of Federal Star Registration (yes, this is for real) at 1–800–544–8814.

A star will be named forever after your chosen one, and a permanent record of the name will be kept in a federal archive register.

# Be a Kid Again

Too often, we let the kid in us get away. Children are a constant reminder of what it's like to be young, and we can recapture the moment by participating in the very games they like to play. How long has it been since the two of you

~ roller-skated

~ played jacks

~ shot marbles

~ swung on a swing

~ rode a bike

Here's my final word of advice on the rejuvenating experience of recapturing lost youth: Go fly a kite.

# Oh, Lovey

This is guaranteed to add some spice to your life. Call your partner by a loving expression you don't usually use:

- ≈ Baby
- ≈ Sweetie
- ≈ Honey
- ≈ Lover
- ≈ Sugar
- ≈ Good lookin'
- ≈ Hot stuff

# Neat Discreet Love

My friend Judy tells me that she and her husband created a special way to say "I love you" in public. One squeezes the other's hand three times. Other signals—winks or coughs—work just as well. But best of all, Judy says, now that she has two children, she has taught them the signal. When she and her son Jody recently were among a group of people waiting for an interview with the school principal, she used the signal to show her confidence in him.

## Reappraising Love

List ten ways that you take your spouse for granted. Sit down and think really hard about what you can do to show your mate how much you care. Then—and this is the hard part— put one new caring way into action each day for the next ten days. Then start the list all over again until it becomes a habit.

## Symbolic Gifts

Gifts that are symbolic of something in your life—a move, a new child, a promotion—always have special meaning. When Harlan's wife, Katherine, who had stayed behind to sell their Kansas City home, finally joined him in New York City, their new hometown, to celebrate their new lives he presented her with a Steuben crystal apple—his way of welcoming her to the Big Apple.

# Savoring Life

I have long observed that my husband and I tend to have our most meaningful, serious talks on the rare occasions when we go out to dinner alone. But eating out can be an expensive way to have a conversation, so I was looking for a way for us to slow down the pace of our lives and make time to share some quiet moments. I began to see how we could create some special time for ourselves last year when we visited Venice, Italy.

The Venetians, like most Europeans, know how to savor life in ways that we Americans seem to have missed. Since space is so limited in their city, they live much of their life outdoors. Venetian families traditionally gather at a piazza after work, where they share a glass of wine or cup of coffee and let the busy day fall away. It's a lovely practice, one that all of us could modify to suit our busy lives.

If your community has an outdoor café, and growing numbers do these days, make it your "special place" and take the time to meet there after work. Do as I do, and call your spouse as often as you can and ask: "Meet at our spot?" Once there, relax and enjoy the moment, however brief, over a quiet glass of wine or seltzer or iced tea.

## Substitute Sweeteners

If your mate shouldn't or can't eat candy, the traditional gift of lovers, fill a candy box with something else that she or he loves—golf balls, mystery novels, cassette tapes, note cards, postcards, or even a nice piece of jewelry.

## Date Night

Make plans to have a regular date with your partner—a special engagement that you virtually never break unless there is an emergency. You could make your date for the first Saturday of each month, or, as one couple I know does, for the first night of a full moon.

Each of you can take turns planning this occasion, which might include a ferry trip, a canoe ride, a Sunday picnic, a getaway to a cottage or a bed-and-breakfast near your home.

## Billet-Doux

Write your partner a romantic note on scented paper. I suggest the lovely French expression, *"Qui vous fait rêver?"* ("What makes you dream?") Tuck it into his or her pocket on Friday morning as you part—a promise for the weekend.

# Loving Our Children
## and Family

Our children are at once our dearest and most maddening possessions. And so great is the responsibility of parenting that we often forget to take—or make—time for enjoying lighthearted, joyous moments with them.

The following pages show you how to make the light moments happen, how to show your children your love and teach them to love others. In short, how to know your children better—as individuals.

In preparing these suggestions, I've especially taken into account the hectic pace of most of our lives, as well as the fact that over 50 percent of all mothers with small children now work. As some of the old traditions, like a glass of milk and cookies with mom after school, fade away, it's my hope that we'll replace the old traditions with some new ones geared to the new structures of our lives.

## The Gift of Time

Years ago, making taffy was cause for a special kind of party called a Taffy Pull. In these days of prepared foods, we've almost forgotten the joy of spending an afternoon in the kitchen. My favorite kitchen companion is my grandchild. Take your child into the kitchen and spend the afternoon together making a cake or brownies or some scrumptious cookies from scratch. If you're truly ambitious, try making candy.

## Take a Ride

Children are so busy learning about the world that they adore things we take utterly for granted. Transportation is just one example. Most small children are thrilled with their first bus, ferry, subway, or trolley car ride. If you want to be more extravagant, consider accompanying a child on a train, plane, or helicopter ride.

# Film Festival

I firmly believe that the families that function best are those that spend time together. A good way to ensure "family" time at least one night a week is to plan a home film festival. Serve popcorn and milk or some other favorite snack, to be eaten in front of the television set, and tune in the VCR to your favorite movies. Add to the fun with a theme:

- Astaire-Rogers

- Tracy-Hepburn

- Great Westerns

- Cartoons

- "The Honeymooners"

- "Upstairs/Downstairs"

- Films about families

- Films about teenagers

Try to invite conversation and comments about the films you watch: how do the characters handle personal setbacks; how do the characters' lives differ from your own; would your children enjoy living in the time or place depicted in the film? Films and videos offer a great way to get to know your children—and for them to understand you.

## Small-Fry Gifts

To amuse a young child, tie a small present such as a whistle or a piece of candy on the outside of a bigger gift.

## Sharing Love

If you're a working parent, you and your children probably miss the intimacy of sharing your day right after school's out. If so, do what my friend Shirley does and leave a tape recorder by the cookie jar. Encourage your kids to talk into it about their day at school, upcoming events, and plans they've made. The tape can serve as a family diary and a calender, but most important, you'll capture the immediate excitement of the day.

## Taking Down the Christmas Tree

Everyone loves putting up the tree, but no one likes taking it down. To inspire your family to do this one last task, tuck small surprise gifts under the tree—to be opened only after the last ornament has been put away and the last needle swept up.

## Make Time for Special Moments

Children, often viewed as a collective unit within the family, hunger to be recognized as individuals. To accomplish this, take each child out alone occasionally, especially if he or she usually has to compete with siblings for your attention. These rare moments alone with your child are a time to get acquainted and really talk with one another.

Make sure the outing is special—lunch at a favorite restaurant when your child is old enough or a trip to the zoo or to some special event.

# Making Book

Reinforce your child's love of reading by giving him or her an especially beautiful, classic book—one with lovely illustrations or a fancy binding.

Here's a list to get you started:

~ *The Adventures of Huckleberry Finn*, by Mark Twain

~ *Alice's Adventures in Wonderland*, by Lewis Carroll

~ *The Story of Dr. Dolittle*, by Hugh Lofting

~ *Pinocchio*, by Carlo Collodi

~ *The Wonderful Wizard of Oz*, by L. Frank Baum

~ *Gulliver's Travels*, by Jonathan Swift

~ *Peter Pan*, by James M. Barrie

~ *Robinson Crusoe*, by Daniel Defoe

~ *Treasure Island*, by Robert Louis Stevenson

~ *The Swiss Family Robinson*, by Johann David Wyss

~ *The Jungle Books*, by Rudyard Kipling

~ *You Come Too*, by Robert Frost

~ *The Sugar-Plum Tree*, by Eugene Field

# Long-Distance Grandparenting

In a time when the average American family moves every five years, and families are typically separated by hundreds if not thousands of miles, many grandparents—as well as aunts and uncles—find themselves maintaining a long-distance relationship with their grandchildren. I've done it myself and have over the years developed some special techniques for keeping in touch.

For one thing, keep in mind that all successful relationships are based on communication. So are these hints:

~ Call often and settle in to talk for a while. Too many of us come from an era when a long-distance call was something special rather than an ordinary occasion, and we basically say our how-are-yous and get off the phone before any kind of real conversation can take shape. But remember, this is a long-distance relationship you're trying for. Since you won't be taking this child out to lunch and to the movies, spend the money on the phone call.

~ Do, however, try to take advantage of the cheaper rates, because once you've established your telephone relationship, you may find yourself listening to a play-by-play description of a trip to Disneyland or a detailed rundown of what happened at Kiddy Kollege last week.

~ Keep a list of things you want to say and questions you

want to ask in order to make the call more meaningful for both of you.

~ End every call with an expression of love.

~ Don't overlook using the mail to further your long-distance friendship. Children love to receive mail, and there are ways to enhance your correspondence with them.

~ Choose stationery with a theme your small friend will enjoy—Charlie Brown, dinosaurs, space ships, animals.

~ Write about what has happened to you—where you've gone and what you've done that might interest a small child. In other words, tell a story or two in your letters. Most important, use the letters to praise your grandchild and tell him or her how proud you are of scholastic, athletic, or other achievements.

~ Send books, audiotapes, and videotapes to your grandchild. These, too, involve communication, and they will give you a further bond and some interesting topics to discuss in your special telephone calls.

~ Finally, when the two of you are about to visit one another, send a calendar marking off the days until you actually will see each other in person.

## Role Reversal

For an interesting and educational family evening, change places—literally—at the dinner table one night. Have each family member assume the role of another. You'll learn a lot about each other, including some ways to show your love a little better.

## Teaching Courage

For the first year or two of a child's life, most are fearless. But gradually, reality sets in and children develop fears—some healthy, some not—about life. To teach your child that good sometimes comes from frightening events, buy him or her a balloon. Write a promissory message—"Good for one movie," "Good for one trip to the zoo,"—and stuff it inside the balloon. Alternatively, stuff a dollar bill inside the balloon. Attach a note telling the child to blow up the balloon until it breaks. Promise him that something good will happen if he does.

## Countdown to the Big Trip

Is the excitement mounting for your next family vacation? Here's a way to have fun and channel it constructively. About ten or fifteen days before you leave, write down on a pad of paper the number of days remaining until Departure Day. Write Day Fifteen on the first sheet, Day Fourteen on the second, and so on. On the reverse side, write down something that the child can do to help get ready for the trip—get the cat's supplies ready, choose some books to take, select his or her clothes, and pick out some favorite toys to take along. Tear off a sheet each day and ask the child to do the appropriate chore.

## You're the One

Each of us likes to feel special and never more so than when we're sick. To make a sick child feel special, keep a particular game—checkers or Chinese checkers—to be brought out and played with only when a child is ill.

## All the Memories Love Can Keep

Create a "memory bank" for each child. It can be as simple as a decorated shoebox or something more elaborate that you decorate yourself or buy. A small trunk filled with one box for each year is ideal.

Begin with a newspaper from the day of the child's birth and add other sentimental mementos—baby shoes, some baby curls, first drawings, an early toy, report cards, special invitations, baby jewelry, lots of photographs. Organize everything, label the box (or boxes), and present the memory trunk to your child at his or her high school graduation party.

# Something Fragile, Something Precious

As an experiment, I once bought a three-year-old child in my life a delicate and somewhat expensive glass bird. A friend who was shopping with me insisted it was an inappropriate gift that would soon be broken, but I couldn't give up the idea that in this age of plastic toys, children could be taught that some things are fragile and important enough to care for in a special way.

I had the bird wrapped in tissue and gift wrapped, so my young friend and I would have to open it carefully. As we studied the bird together, I explained that it was a different kind of present. That since it could easily break he would have to handle it with care and put it in a special place when he wasn't looking at it. This wasn't a toy that could be played with, I said, but rather, something precious to hold and admire.

Imagine my delight when I visited the child's first apartment some twenty years later and saw the bird, all in one piece, accorded a place of honor.

## Bedtime Story

Tape-record a favorite childhood book—in your voice—and give it to your child on a special occasion or when you will be out of town for a few days.

## Have I Hugged You Yet Today?

I've observed that adults often solicit hugs and kisses from small children, but rarely do we offer a hug on unequivocal terms—so the child feels he has received something rather than given it. But turnabout's fair play. So today, don't ask your favorite child for a hug. Ask if you can give him one.

## They're Playing Your Song

Find a copy of a song that has your child's name and teach it to him or her. It will be her special song, and you can sing it on long car trips and on special occasions like her birthday. Having a special song helps a child develop a sense of identity. Some songs to consider are: "Wake Up, Little Susie" (a fifties hit); "Louise" (often sung by Maurice Chevalier); "Mary"; "Li'l Liza Jane"; and "Katie Did" (an old Stephen Foster tune).

## Bake a Promise Cake

Bake your children a special "promise" cake. Use a favorite recipe or even a cake mix. Write out special messages, such as "Trip to buy favorite $5 toy" or "Trip to movie." Wrap the promises in foil, taking care to make the packages large enough to see, and add them to the cake batter just before you pour it into the baking pans.

# When Someone You Love Can't Come Home for Christmas

When someone you love can't come home for Christmas, you can send Christmas to him or her instead, as one family I know did during Operation Desert Storm. Gather the family a few weeks before Christmas and hold a pre-Christmas party. Make sure the tree is up to add atmosphere when you do this. Videotape people greeting one another as they arrive, talking around the dinner table, and singing carols. Let individuals send their Christmas wishes. Finally, send the tape off to the missing family member so he or she will get it in time for Christmas.

# A Stitch for All Time

Here's something special to do when the family is all together for a holiday dinner: Set the table with a white tablecloth and give people pencils or felt-tipped pens. Encourage them to write a personal message and sign their names. Embroider the writing later to make it permanent. In the center, stitch the event and the date. The tablecloth will become a treasured family memento that you will want to use at other family gatherings.

This tablecloth also makes a special moving day or shower gift for a close friend. It's a sort of modern-day friendship quilt.

# Think Back

The next time you're meeting a long-lost sibling and want to mark the occasion with a small gift, think back to the time you grew up together. Did you buy penny candy together on weekends? Fly kites? Go to baseball games? Such shared experiences can be the inspiration for unusual gifts.

My friend Irene often laughingly recalls the time she traveled by train from the Midwest to the West Coast with two of her children to greet their elder brother's tall ship, the *Eagle*, which was arriving in San Francisco after a four-month cruise around Australia. For years, the children had received boxes of their favorite Girl Scout cookies as a spring vacation present, and this year was no exception. Irene and the two children had toted their brother's favorite cookies half a continent.

The family was joyously reunited, and when they began to share their presents, they were amazed and amused to discover that the gift of Girl Scout cookies was mutual. The family sailor had met two Australian Girl Scouts aboard ship and had purchased cookies for his siblings. Between them, their cookies had collectively traveled halfway around the world to reach their recipients.

# Here's to You, Too

When my friend Joan received from her sister-in-law a card whose cover read, "Birthday wishes for my favorite perfectionist," she wasn't sure what to think. But all was well when she saw that the inside of the card said: "Takes one to know one." She even admired her sister-in-law's forthrightness.

The next year, on a whim, she sent the card back to her sister-in-law, who enjoyed the joke.

The next year, she got the card back again.

For twenty years, the two women have been trading off the same birthday card.

Recycling tip: When you find something good, use it over and over.

## Family Heirlooms

When former Miss America Mary Ann Mobley had her little girl, husband Gary Collins bought a tiny bathing suit inscribed "Future Miss America." When the little beauty outgrew her first suit, Mary Ann had it framed and gave it to Daddy. It hangs in his office today.

Another friend once told me that after her father died, her mother had a beautiful jacket that he had worn to a costume ball as a young man framed for her to keep forever.

Don't forget: Family heirlooms are often what you make of them.

## Making History

Give your teenager a tape recorder and the assignment to sit down and interview his grandparents about their lives and the family history. It's a wonderful bonding experience for them all, and you'll all treasure the tape in years to come. In fact, in one family I know, the tape has become something of a best-seller—with everyone who hears it asking for a copy.

## A Promise to Return

Leaving your children while you travel? Make plans to leave them a small gift for each day of your absence—something to let them know you're thinking of them. If you number the gifts, countdown fashion, to the day of your return, they will also be a reminder of when you can be reunited.

Your child's caretaker can present the gifts at a special time each day—bedtime, snacktime, or even at a moment when the child is feeling low and missing you.

## Special Thoughts

My friends Mary and Kevin bought special blank books, one for each family member. Every year on New Year's Eve, they gather together and write loving Christmas messages in each other's books.

# Happy Half Birthday

The Jamesons celebrate half birthdays. Joanie first got the idea when her youngest daughter, Beth, was born near Christmas. Joanie felt that Beth would always feel a little shortchanged, having a birthday so close to Christmas. So she arranged for a half-birthday party. The idea stuck, the other two children demanded the same, and now the family routinely and riotously celebrates everyone's half birthday.

Joanie says these are family-only occasions. She bakes half a birthday cake, and decorates it with half a candle. Everyone wears half-birthday hats and tries to come up with funny "half" presents. One year one sibling gave Beth some jacks; another gave her a ball.

# A Measure of Time

Each year, for your child's birthday, write a birthday letter recording the highlights of the past year through your child's eyes—the ups and downs, the achievements, even the setbacks that do so much to build character. Keep the letters until your child is eighteen or for some other big occasion. Then tie them with a satin ribbon, buy a decorative box for them if you wish, and present them to your child.

## Room to Grow

The most joyful houses are those that are filled with the signs of real people living life to the fullest. That's why I've continued and even elaborated upon a custom my own family started when my sister and I were children. As soon as each of my children grew old enough to be interested in measuring himself, I let him do so against a kitchen wall. With a yardstick, we marked the annual progress right on the wall. I made a pencil mark when we measured, and later used a felt-tip pen (a different color for each child) to write in the year and the height. Across the top of each permanent measurement, I wrote each child's name and decorated it with whimsical stickers. Even though none of my children lives at home anymore, their personal yardsticks have not been painted over.

## Finding Love in All the Funny Places

When your children are bickering, and you can't stand it any more, assign them to the task of washing windows. Just be sure to put one child on each side of the window. It's guaranteed—smiles and monkeyshines will soon break out.

# Loving Our Parents

*O*nly fifty years ago, most of us could expect to lose a parent by the time we reached adulthood. Today, our parents are with us longer, and are more in need of special attention than they have ever been. Fiftieth wedding anniversaries, once rare, have become commonplace. Ninetieth and even one-hundredth birthdays are celebrated more often these days and, one hopes, with the fanfare and extraordinary love they merit.

Loving our parents is both easier and more difficult than it has been for past generations. As we pass through new and more extended life phases, we have had to learn new ways of relating to our parents. As society has changed over the past decades, the traditional respect that was shown for generations to the elderly has declined, to be replaced with new customs and ways of showing respect. We have also had an opportunity to become closer to our parents as we put our newfound psychological skills, a positive by-product of our age, to work.

Too often, these days, our care of the elderly is directed toward making their lives more comfortable, and in this section, you'll find plenty of helpful suggestions to guide you in doing just that. But I've also focused on some of the spiritual and emotional ways you can enhance your loving relationship with your parents—showing them that you love them, and letting them show their love for you.

# How Does Your Garden Grow?

My friend Margaret makes a pilgrimage every spring to her mother's Springfield, Illinois, home in order to plant her mother's garden. She knows a gardener could be hired for the task but says that would diminish the "brag" value of what she does, that is, the pleasure her mother derives all summer from telling anyone who passes by: "My daughter comes home every year to plant this for me."

# A Very Special Gift

Ma Bell can provide you with a very special gift for your parents. For a major birthday or anniversary, arrange for a conference call with some special people in your parents' lives—the members of their wedding party, their siblings, old war buddies, or old high school or college chums.

Call your long-distance service and ask about conference calls—how to set one up, when the rates are lowest. Contact the people whom you want to participate and set a time that's agreeable to all. (It's not always easy to get everyone to agree to a time, but it's easier than getting them together at a specific place.) Then make sure your loved ones are home to receive the call. It's a surprise they'll always treasure.

# A Trip Down Nostalgia Lane

Treat an elderly friend or relative to a subscription to her hometown or girlhood newspaper. Shut-ins will treasure this as a unique way to keep up with old friends and memories, but most elderly persons will enjoy reading about what's happening in a favorite place from their past.

# Making a Date for Love

When my friend Kathy moved back to the town where she had grown up, her grandmother looked forward to seeing a great deal of her favorite granddaughter—more of her in fact than Kathy's busy work schedule permitted her to give. Kathy solved the problem by making a standing lunch date with her grandmother every Wednesday. Soon, both women found themselves looking forward to their time together and rarely cancelled the engagement.

If you have a relative who makes demands on your time, try setting aside a regular period to meet. Older persons especially appreciate the regularity of a standing date. You can add importance to these occasions by giving your family member a large, colorful wall calendar marked with your regular meeting times as well as the holidays you will be sharing.

# Memories Are Made of This

Combine into one master videotape all the old home movies of your parents when they were young, their wedding, and other important events in their lives with newer videotapes of you and your siblings as children, your weddings, and other important events.

There are video-editing businesses that can edit your tapes and merge film and videotape into one master tape. Present this to your parents on a special occasion.

# The Power of the Written Word

I was deeply touched one day to open my mail and find this lovely note from my godson Scott:

> *Dear Godparents,*
> *If I knew God's address, I would write to him to say make more godparents like you.*

I'll always treasure the note, not least because it is handwritten. The art of letter writing is rapidly becoming a lost one, but you can instill the habit in your children. Encourage them to write thank-you notes and special letters to grandparents and other family members and friends by providing them with a supply of colorful stationery and pens. Make letter-writing a fun experience and a special occasion.

# Twenty-five Reasons We Love You

For your parents' twenty-fifth wedding anniversary, make a special anniversary book. Buy twenty-five beautiful sheets of paper to use on the book's inside pages and some colorful ones for the covers. You'll need one inside page for every year of marriage.

On each inside page write one example of a way your parents have shown love toward you. Try to make the examples specific, and don't worry if any one episode doesn't represent a major sacrifice. It's all the little sacrifices your parents made for you that add up to the major ones. Here are some examples:

"The way you took care of me when I had the measles."

"The way you always cooked our favorite foods on Friday night."

"The toy sewing machine you gave me for my eighth birthday."

On one of the cover pages, write the title: "Twenty-five Reasons We Love You." Tie the pages together with a pretty ribbon and present the book at the party for the guests of honor.

For an added special touch, hire a calligrapher to "write" the book for you.

# A Basketful of Love

What to give your parents or grandparents who have everything and then some? My mavens report that seniors love edibles, and I've had great success in sending baskets full of special goodies to the seniors I know. Among my favorite choices are teas, coffees, good cookies and biscuits, chocolates, special baked and canned delicacies.

A special hint: think about enclosing some "ethnic" foods. They are often especially appreciated.

# Comfort Presents

Watch elderly relatives to see what you can give them that will make their lives more comfortable or, for that matter, safer. When a friend's mother began to suffer from poor circulation, her mother didn't realize that she needed extra-thick pot holders to use when she cooked. After the visit, my friend bought her mother some, wrapped them in cheerful no-occasion paper, and enclosed a little note explaining the purpose of the gift. She told her how proud she was that she was still able to live alone at age ninety-one. She vowed to do everything she could to help her continue her life the way she wanted it, and said that she thought these pot holders would help keep her safer in the kitchen.

On another occasion, when she noticed her mother had trouble dialing the telephone because her eyesight had failed, she sent her a telephone with overscale buttons. On each occasion the mother was thrilled with the attention and the gifts and proudly showed them off to anyone who visited her.

Once I caught on to my friend's methods, I discovered countless items in stores and mail-order catalogs that can add to someone's comfort. Check out local stores and order some of the catalogs designed to aid handicapped persons. In one source alone, I found a pen designed to help arthritic fingers write more easily, an array of pillows to ease tender parts of the body, and a clock that projects the time—in large numerals—on the ceiling in a darkened room.

# A Family Get-Together Especially for Grandma

When it became obvious that my grandmother could travel only with difficulty to visit various members of the family, I decided we should go to her. That's when I organized our annual family picnic weekend at her house. Family members now travel from Ohio, Nebraska, New York, and Florida for Grandma's annual get-together.

We all bring dishes we've made at home or purchased from our favorite hometown food stores. Anyone who lives too far away to bring anything shops locally and cooks in Grandma's kitchen.

Like most women of her generation, Grandma isn't completely comfortable with a party at her house where she isn't expected to pitch in, if not direct the operations in their entirety. To solve this problem, we declared her the guest of honor and insisted that she do nothing but enjoy herself. We decorated a special chair for her to sit on, with streamers and balloons—and then insisted that she sit in it while we worked, although we soon learned that a few tactful consultations with her also helped make her feel important.

# Special Outings

Arrange a special outing for your favorite elderly person to visit a beloved relative or friend. I learned how much such visits can mean when I asked a great-aunt who got around fine for day-to-day errands but no longer took long car trips by herself if there was anything special I could do for her. She confessed that a favorite cousin whom she had spent many happy times with in childhood was about to enter a nursing home, and she wanted to visit with her one more time in the cousin's home. The cousin lived eighty miles away. I promptly made the arrangements, delivered my aunt to her cousin's doorstep, feigned an errand in town, and left the two women alone for several hours.

Three years later, my aunt has not stopped talking about what a great favor this was to her, and since then, I've also arranged several other such outings. She never directly asks me to take her anywhere but occasionally drops into our conversations the fact that so-and-so is moving to Florida or leaving the state to live with her children. So far, I've always been able to arrange a visit, and the pleasure we both get from these excursions is truly immeasurable.

An added benefit is that my aunt and I have become much better acquainted through our long drives. She's often in a nostalgic mood on the way home, and I'm an eager listener.

# Old-Time Presents

Give your favorite oldster what I like to call an "old-time" present—something that's not especially common today that he or she will nevertheless appreciate, in part for the memories it generates. My favorite "old-time" present is mono-grammed cloth handkerchiefs for men and delicately embroi-dered ones for women.

I gave a favorite cousin whose trademark was his dapper style of dressing a bow tie. He said he hadn't had one in years and was delighted when I told him they were making a comeback.

In a similar vein, I found a lovely satin bed jacket for another elderly friend.

I've also given friends and family members a nightshirt, a woman's Victorian watch fob, and a man's pocket watch, and for reasons too involved to explain here, a pair of fire-engine red long johns. Suffice it to say that the idea for the latter gift came from a conversation with the eventual recipi-ent.

Listen carefully when an older person you know remi-nisces, and you'll get some helpful clues to "old-time" gifts.

## Old Photos, Old Love

Find and buy an old photograph that has special meaning to someone you love. Perhaps it will be the opera house in the town where your mother grew up, or Main Street in a town where she lived as a young married woman.

Old photos often show up at flea markets or you can occasionally buy copy prints from local historical societies.

If the print is black-and-white, have a sepia-tinted copy made and buy a nice wood frame to complement it.

One friend of mine had a series of photos framed showing every house her parents had ever lived in.

## Greetings from Your President

The President and First Lady will send special greetings to persons eighty-five and older and those couples celebrating their fiftieth wedding anniversary. Send requests to the Greetings Dept., Old Executive Office Building, Room 39, Washington, DC 20500. Allow four weeks.

# Loving Our Friends, Colleagues, and Acquaintances

*I*n an era where few of us are fortunate enough to live near our families, our friends have become more valuable than ever. They are, quite literally, substitute families, people who care for us and nurture us when our real families aren't around to do so. And even those of us who come from close families realize that friends provide an extra source of support, an added barrier against the world.

Valuable though our friends may be, in our frantically busy lives we too often take them for granted. We rarely get together, and when we do sit down to talk, the conversation often turns to how little time we have for anything—including friendship.

This past New Year's Eve, I resolved to spend more time with my friends, and to indulge them—and me—in the little gestures that do so much to breathe life into tired relationships. I'm proud to say that unlike most New Year resolutions, I've kept this one—and the reward has been enormous. Friends have come back into my life, and I in theirs in many wonderful ways. What I've done is easily accessible to you, and to anyone who wants to renew old friendships. I hope the suggestions on the following pages help you get started on this wonderful journey.

# Keeping Up

No time to keep up with friends? It's a complaint I hear more and more often. Remember, you don't have to see someone every week or spend an hour on the phone with them every day to let them know you care about them and are thinking of them.

One way I keep in touch is to send clippings and magazine articles to friends whenever I think I've found something of special interest. This week, I sent a clipping about his university to a young man who had just graduated. I sent an editorial page cartoon to a friend who's politically active, and I sent a comic strip that I knew would amuse her to an old college friend.

## Hostess Gifts

Instead of taking the traditional wine or flowers, I'm always looking for something unusual to give as hostess gifts. When I find something that's right, I stock up on it, thus saving myself a little time. Some of my favorites have been a hardwood orange peeler that's truly beautiful and some wittily shaped ceramic spoon rests. I also buy unusually flavored vinegars (try champagne and raspberry) and fancy jams to give as hostess presents.

## Holiday Rush

Most of us, that is, most of us over the age of consent, experience the Christmas-Chanukah-New Year's holidays at least in part with some ambivalence, usually because we have so much to do. Thus we should take extra care of each other at this time of the year.

When you see a friend struggling with an array of tasks, offer to take something off her hands. Perhaps you can wrap Christmas presents for her, or entertain her child for an afternoon so she can go shopping. And if you're lucky, your friend will reciprocate—and maybe you can even trade off the two tasks each of you dislike most.

# Ask Someone for Something

In our go-it-alone world, we tend to see it as a sign of weakness to ask someone for a favor, even when we badly need one. But asking a friend or partner to do something for you makes the other person feel important and needed. It's a self-esteem raiser.

I learned to ask for favors the hard way when I was a young wife struggling to maintain a household and rear my children. I wanted my husband to come home to a perfect house and perfect children every night. He offered to help out—by bringing home a carry out dinner or doing the grocery shopping on the way home from work—but I wouldn't let him. Finally, when I could cope no longer, I asked him to run a few errands, and to my surprise, he appeared eager to help.

Then I took matters one step further and couched my requests by first saying, "I really need to ask you for a favor." He positively beamed. And I learned the beauty of receiving as well as giving.

# High Time for Tea

My mother always used to put up a pot of tea whenever anything went wrong in someone's life, and that's a good idea, but I've discovered the joy of serving tea on happier, calmer occasions as well. The small late-afternoon meal that the British have long indulged in has its special rewards.

Make the tea from scratch, using loose tea or tea bags, and serve it from a teapot. There's a soothing, calming quality about the ritual of pouring tea from a teapot. Use your best china, your best silver, and napkins.

Serve scones or muffins, something sweet but not cloyingly so, and a few good jams or perhaps a lemon curd spread. If it's available you may even want to try clotted cream, another British specialty, on your scones.

Once you have a hot cup of tea nestled in your hand, sit back and leisurely begin to catch up on your lives.

# Windowbox View

Put together a colorful windowbox for a shut-in or elderly person who doesn't get out much—and then take care of it if necessary.

## Things to Do with $1

Drop it on the street and imagine the pleasure it will give someone to find it.

~ Send a card to someone with whom you've lost touch.

~ Buy a small plant or one showy flower to give to a friend.

~ Donate it to the first cause you see. (Small stores, especially drugstores, often have collection jars for various charities.)

~ Add it to someone's regular tip.

When you're generous with someone else, the good feeling inside you expands until it bursts and touches those around you.

# Bedside Manners

With modern medicine being what it is, we're fortunate that most hospital visits these days are made to friends who aren't very sick, who will be recuperating quickly, or who, if we're really lucky, have just given birth, a particularly joyous kind of visit.

Until recently I've never had occasion to visit someone who is seriously ill and unlikely to recover, but this is something more of us will face, I fear, in the coming years as we cope with the changes in our society brought about by AIDS and the growing elderly population.

In visiting with very ill friends, I have learned that a different set of bedside manners is called for, and I want to share this with you.

Don't feel you must talk. A really ill person may not be able or willing to talk, but he or she will still take comfort in just knowing you are there.

Do touch. It's more difficult than you would imagine to touch someone hooked up to ten intravenous lines and a respirator, but human contact is what sick people need most. Hold your friend's hand and touch his face. Some people find foot massage relaxing. Others want their arms and legs exercised gently. (Check with a nurse if you are unsure whether this will be okay for your friend.)

If your friend can't speak, ask him to squeeze your hand to answer questions—one squeeze is no, two is yes. But even with this kind of conversation, take care not to overdo it.

Consider giving your friend a tape player and some quiet,

soul-soothing music to drown out the sounds of the technology used in modern medicine.

Bring small appropriate gifts. Flowers may not be allowed, but scented lotions and creams or a good lip balm can provide a different kind of relief. A small potpourri to scent the sickroom is wonderful, provided your friend is not suffering from a respiratory ailment.

Take a small object for your friend to hold. I recently bought some *santos* made in the Philippines—small, old wooden saints. They are about four inches high—the perfect size to grasp. Greek worry beads are another hand-holding gift, as is a cool marble egg or a small ceramic animal.

Help to take care of the family members who are standing by. As a friend you will probably come and go, but family members may be maintaining a round-the-clock vigil. Take newspapers, magazines, cookies or muffins, anything that will help them get through the long hours of waiting.

Finally, take your cues from the family about discussing the illness. They may be in a state of denial, unable to speak realistically about what is going on—or they may need a comforting shoulder when reality sets in. Try to give them what they need.

# A Time to Send Money

Ordinarily I avoid giving gifts of money. To my way of thinking, it isn't as personal as a handpicked present. But there is one time when money may turn out to be a special treat, and that is when a friend is having a second or third child. Consider this: She undoubtedly already has much of the equipment she needs for a baby, and there will be lots of hand-me-downs. But there is probably also something special she would like for this baby. A check, accompanied by a note suggesting this to her, is an especially considerate present.

# Share Your Bounty

If you garden, like most people you may find that your garden baskets runneth over in late summer, when everything you've planted ripens at the same time. Rather than letting all the fruits and vegetables go to waste (and few of us take the time to can these days), do what one senior citizens group does and set up a "bounty table." Leave extra produce and fruit on a roadside table for anyone who wants or needs it.

## Thinking of You

Don't save postcards for when you're on vacation. Use them year-round as a way to keep in touch with friends and family. Everyone loves to get mail, and postcards are easier to write than letters. You'll have the fun of collecting the cards—and even more fun when you send them off.

Set yourself up so you always have everything you need to send the cards: Keep a cache of funny or pretty cards, brightly colored pens, and postcard stamps on hand at all times.

## A Small Treasure

Make some baby clothes for a friend's new baby. I once attended a shower where the most charming present was a small layette of hand-sewn baby clothes. They were sewn in soft white flannel, and blanket-stitched in pale yellow and green. If time permits, use cross-stitch to add the baby's name and birthdate to one item, such as a flannel receiving blanket. As the child gets a little older, this can become a cherished item.

## A Hand-Tailored Gift of Love

Create a special basket for a friend who's ill or otherwise indisposed. Decorate the basket with ribbons and fill it with small presents—a paperback book, a specially scented hand lotion, some note cards, scented soaps, a decorative comb or some other interesting object. When choosing items for the basket, keep in mind the recipient's age and interests.

## Keeping in Touch

When a friend moves, her heart will still be with her old home and friends—at least until she begins to make new friends. Help someone through the transition period by saving clips from the local newspaper. When you have enough of them to make a healthy-size package, send them, along with a chatty letter, to her. They will cheer her up and let her know she is not forgotten.

# A Warm Send-off

Plan a farewell party for a friend who's moving. Ask everyone to bring the name of someone who lives near her new hometown—a contact to help her get started in her new life. (For those who can't bring a contact, suggest a travel or history book about her new home. Most parts of the country have books written about them, and many have specialized books on hiking, famous gardens, a nearby city.)

As a collective gift, fill in a date book with all your names and addresses and give it to her.

# Ours Forever

Sharing cements a friendship like nothing else. My friends and I have devised an unusual means of sharing our possessions that adds a new dimension to both our belongings and our friendships.

Our unusual sharing pattern began when I admired a battered old T-shirt that my friend Susan wore. Its charm was in its logo: "Mayor Daley's Youth Corps." I, a former Chicagoan, was wildly envious. Susan finally parted with the shirt, leaving it and a funny note (about our advancing ages, I'm sorry to say) on the guest bed after one of her annual visits.

But I knew she missed it. So two years later, after a few carefully selected wearings, I shipped it back to her. Imagine my surprise, when in another two years, she sent it back to me. I know what to do with it in two more years.

I recently worked out another long-term loan that gives me great satisfaction. When I saw Marie in a stunning black print dress, I knew that a fringed silk shawl I had bought years ago at a Paris flea market would be the perfect topper for it. I had never been able to bring my solidly unflamboyant self to wear the shawl with its flamboyant six-inch fringe, but have always thought it a shame that something so beautiful hung in my closet year in and year out. Explaining that I couldn't bear to part with it permanently, I suggested to Marie that she take it on a long-term loan. She loves it even more than I do, and looks more stunning in it, too. And I get the satisfaction of knowing that a beautiful object, owned by me, is put to good use.

Moral: Use it or lose it. But consider losing it—temporarily—to a friend.

## Give the Gift of Time

Offer to run a friend's Saturday errands at a time when you know he is particularly busy or burdened.

## Perfection in Small Packages

It is in nature that we often find the most sublime and simple forms of perfection. Some of these can be shared with others:

~ a perfect bouquet of ordinary summer flowers such as zinnias and marigolds

~ a perfect bag of homegrown tomatoes

~ a perfect huge spray of forsythia

~ a perfect small spray of bittersweet

## Consoling Help

"Let me be your 911." Send a recently bereaved friend a note specifically telling her you'd like to be her 911 for a while. Say you hope she'll call whenever she needs to talk. When she does, give her the gift of patience—and listen for as long as she needs you to.

## Welcome to Our World

An old custom worthy of revival is that of delivering a home-cooked, usually baked, treat to a new neighbor. Neighbors used to introduce themselves to someone new by taking over a pie or cake. It was traditionally delivered not on a paper plate but in a dish or pan—thus giving the new neighbor a reason to call on you. The dish had to be returned! And the two visits were usually enough to start a budding friendship.

# Personalized Travel Journal

Give a friend who's embarking on a trip a travel journal so she can record all her happy memories. There are books especially designed for this purpose, but they're often hardback (too heavy) and too small (those little diary-size pages just won't do when you're describing the Taj Mahal or Chartres).

Experienced travelers head to stationery stores to buy larger-size lined notebooks—often the kind that schoolkids carry. Buy one for a friend and customize it with a paper pocket for maps and travel information. Attach a pen with a pretty ribbon.

# Taking Time to Help

Make a date with an elderly or infirm friend for a special holiday outing—a Christmas shopping expedition with the emphasis on her needs and then a leisurely tea or lunch afterward. Your friend gets needed help with her shopping, and the pleasure of your company—and undivided attention.

## Just Say "Well Done"

Whenever a friend achieves a special success—finishes a big project or gets a much-wanted promotion—take time to handwrite a congratulatory note. Likewise, when a friend does not get something he or she has striven for, send along a note acknowledging the disappointment—and the hard work that went into the project. Your note will be a mood brightener on an otherwise momentarily gloomy horizon.

## Birthday Book

Make or buy a birthday book for a friend *and* collect and write in all the important birthdays in her life before giving it to her.

# Don't Buy the Biggest, Buy the Best

Buy friends small gifts but flatter them by buying the very best. Some suggestions:

~ A natural-bristle brush

~ Top-of-the-line comb

~ Sable paintbrushes

~ Silver thimble

~ Leather garden gloves

~ Linen handkerchiefs

# Owner's Manual for Your House

Selling your house? Do the house and the new owner a good turn. Write an owner's manual that describes how to operate the dishwasher, air conditioner, and other major appliances, how the heating system works, how the fuse box works (and where it is). Leave the names of your favorite plumber, electrician, and other service persons.

# Welcome Home, Baby

When friends or relatives are at the hospital bringing home their new baby, take advantage of their absence to decorate their yard as a way of greeting the new arrival and also letting friends and neighbors who pass by learn the good news. Hang a banner that announces "It's a boy" or "It's a girl," and tie appropriately colored ribbons around the yard.

This joyful custom has been growing in various parts of the country for several years now. I've known grandparents to decorate their doors, or in rural areas, their mailboxes, to announce the good news to the neighborhood. And one rural postman I know, a first-time grandpa, bedecked his car with blue ribbons to announce the new arrival to all on his mail route.

When you decorate someone's yard, don't forget to take a picture for Baby's memory book.

## Saying Good-bye in Style

When a friend is moving away, help her get acquainted with her new home. As soon as you know she's moving, write the Chamber of Commerce and tourist bureau to request information. The information you receive from these sources should lead you to still more sources. Call the local telephone company and order telephone directories. (Get both the white and yellow pages.) Contact an art museum, zoo, or other public institution in her new community and order a canvas tote bag. Failing this, order a shopping bag from a big department store in her new hometown. Pack all the information into the bag you've found and present it to your friend.

## Being There

Most of us are around to comfort a friend who has lost a loved one, but then we tend to leave one another alone once the formal period of mourning—a wake or *shiva* period—is over. Yet I believe that's the very time when our friends most need us and are least prepared to reach out to us.

To ease friends through this difficult period, I send a plant or small bouquet along with a note that simply says, "Thinking of you."

If I feel comfortable doing so, I call and ask to deliver my gift in person. It gives me a chance to check up on the person and let him or her know that I and his other friends are still there for him.

# Grand Gestures

## A Day at the Races

A friend's boss wins kudos for a special treat she gave her staff of ten. This real estate broker took her entire staff to the Santa Ana racetrack, where they were seated at the best trackside table in the dining room. As the *coup de grâce*, each person found an envelope containing one hundred dollars in betting money at her place.

## Her Personal Best

Brooke Shields wrote to tell me about a moment she considers her grandest gesture:

"When I was fourteen, I asked my Mom to get help about her drinking. It was the best 'I love you' I'll ever say."

## Special Places

A man I know planned an extravagant trip for his wife's fortieth birthday. He whisked her off for two sybaritic weeks, one in each of her two favorite cities, San Francisco and New York. The day after they arrived at each of their destinations, she was treated to a rejuvenating spa day at a well-known beauty salon to help her work off jet lag. The rest of the time was filled with her favorite activities: attending the theater and the ballet, shopping, and taking long walks around her special cities.

## Sharing Your Love

When you've given each other everything, it's time to share your love with the larger world. For their fiftieth wedding anniversary, my friends Henry and Doris commissioned a large batik wall hanging by an established community artist and donated it to their synagogue, where it hangs in a place of honor in the community room.

## Small but Grand Ways to Spoil a Loved One

I recently availed myself of the opportunity for an all-too-rare visit with my sister—a brief side trip from my usually busy travel schedule promoting my books and etiquette schools. I was so touched when she brought me home from the airport, handed me a glass of chilled wine and, without a word, went into her bathroom to draw me a warm, scented bath. Fresh towels and soap were laid out, a small table held a bouquet and room for my wineglass, and the bathroom was entirely candlelit. But best of all, on the steamy mirror she had written: "Welcome, Sis."

## More Is Better

A well-known professional golfer, who is too modest to let me use her name, has a reputation among her friends for her caring attention. She frequently visits ill friends, often sends flowers and small presents, and is especially partial to greeting cards. She seems to believe, in fact, that if one card is good, many cards are better. Family and friends' birthdays often warrant three or four cards and, to date, she has sent fifty-three get-well cards to another professional golfer, a young woman who is battling cancer.

# Specially Made

In the fifty years of their marriage, my grandfather, a stern, no-nonsense man, limited his gift giving to important occasions in my grandmother's life—birthdays and anniversaries, to be exact. Thus, you can imagine everyone's surprise when he went out of his way—and secretively, too—to plan a very special present during the forty-third year of their marriage.

My grandparents were undertaking their annual visit from Illinois to visit their son in California—traveling by train, as usual, because my grandmother declined to go any other way. My grandfather, who regularly flew to Chicago on business and loved long driving trips, went by train only grudgingly and was capable of grousing his way across the continent.

Imagine my grandmother's chagrin—and even, she later admitted, her fear that my grandfather had abandoned her to make the trip alone—when my grandfather mysteriously vanished for almost an hour during their layover in Chicago. All was forgiven, though, when my grandfather returned and presented her with a small black velvet box.

In it was a ring he had designed himself and commissioned a jeweler to make: three diamonds surrounded by delicately drooping gold daisy petals—a special tribute if you knew her nickname was Daisy.

The ring, which has had a colorful history (it once was lost for ten years, only to be rediscovered in a sugar bowl), gave me the idea for this part of the book. I never tire of hearing the story, and I tell it to my own children whenever I wear the ring.

# A Memory Tree

In my family we started a custom when we had our first child that we have continued with our grandchildren. With the arrival of each child, we plant a tree that will grow along with the child. Even though my children no longer live at home, I can still look out my kitchen window and see the Billy Oak, the Jackie Willow, and the Erin Apple.

When the beloved grandfather of our good friends, the Snieskis, died, our son Billy asked us to send them a tree that could be planted in the man's memory. The Snieskis love the tree and say it warms their hearts to look out their window and see a permanent memorial to their departed grandfather.

More recently when I was at a loss for a housewarming gift for special friends, I took a chance and had a nursery send them a tree. When Carol called me, practically in tears, to thank me for the tree, I knew I'd found another use for our tree-planting custom. Here are some good trees to consider:

### Small—Twenty to Twenty-five Feet

~ Flowering crab apple—fast growing, ornamental

~ Eastern redbud—moderate growth, dark green foliage

~ Common sassafras—moderate growth, spectacular fall color, but not always readily available

### *Medium—Forty to Sixty Feet*

~ Thornless honey locust—fast growing, small leaves

~ Red maple—fast growing, exceptional fall color, good city tree

~ White ash—moderate growth, colorful

### *Large—Seventy to Eighty-five Feet*

~ London plane—fast growing, looks like a sycamore but is disease resistant

~ Tulip poplar—fast growing, great shade

~ White and red oak—slow growing, spectacular red leaves each fall

## Fly Away with Me

I was recently delighted to watch one good friend of mine give a magnificent gift to another friend.

Janie had had a horrendous year by anyone's standards—full of stress over work and the loss of a loved one. Shana, a frequent flyer, had accumulated thousands of free travel miles through her work as a lawyer. She told Janie to meet her at the airport with a suitcase packed full of enough warm-weather clothes to last a week. Shana and Janie flew off to St. Thomas for a lazy week of lounging in the sun, sipping tropical drinks, and eating healthful food.

## The Key to Happiness

When Rita Moreno and her husband bought their first home together, he gave her a gold key with a note that said: "Here is the key to our home and my heart."

## And Now, a Word from Some Special People

I read about a brother who gave his sister the most wonderful college graduation gift. He wrote twenty of the people whom she admired most and enclosed a note, with a pre-addressed, stamped envelope, asking them to please send a congratulatory note to his sister. When the first note—from her favorite female vocalist—arrived, she called to berate him for playing a cruel joke on her. She did the same thing after the second note from a favorite rock singer. When notes arrived from Justice Sandra Day O'Connor and James Taylor and Billy Joel, she began to see the light—and the love.

## Gallantry

In the ultimate thank-you gesture, President Ronald Reagan used to send flowers to his mother-in-law on Nancy Reagan's birthday.

# Flowers For All

I once read that Eileen McKenney, the infamous vamp immortalized during the 1930s in the book and later the Broadway play *My Sister Eileen*, took offense at a paltry, unsightly corsage sent by an aspiring beau. Not one to suffer slights gladly, she walked over to her local, friendly florist and exchanged—well, upgraded—her purple disaster to a lovely white orchid. Now *that* was a woman who expected to have flowers in her life.

Time and changing customs have diminished our expectations, no doubt, and these days, most of us don't expect flowers on a regular enough basis to be picky, à la Eileen.

Some of us, though, never get flowers at all. In my book, these are the most deserving souls of all. That's why I think we should consider sending flowers, be they a lavish bouquet or a single delicate orchid, to someone who may never have received such a gift before.

On my list of friends whose lives were recently enhanced by the arrival of an unexpected spray of posies: a friend who's blind (he can't see them, but he can smell and touch them); an eleven-year-old friend who's first and only pet died recently. You must have your own list. All you need to do is contact your local FTD florist to arrange for your own special delivery.

## Future Returns

Robert is not only happily married to my friend June but also has made it absolutely clear that he intends to stay that way. On their tenth anniversary, he arranged for four cases of a very fine French wine to be delivered to his wife with a note that read: "This wine needs to age for about ten years, which means it will be perfect to drink on our twentieth anniversary—at a large party we'll be giving for all our friends to celebrate our love. Here's to another ten years of constant love."

## A Banner Day

When Don's mother turned eighty-five, knowing that she was proud of her age, he made arrangements for a banner to fly across Main Street in the small Iowa town where she lived. It read: "Happy Eighty-fifth Birthday, Sarah Jones." It hung proudly throughout her birthday and generated lots of excitement in her normally quiet life. She happily reported that once the banner went up, her telephone never stopped ringing.

If your birthday honoree is sensitive about his or her age, you might want to be tactful and omit any mention of age.

# On the Bench Where We Met

Marie and Jack claim they fell in love sitting on a park bench.

Before leaving for their honeymoon, Jack made arrangements to have a park bench just like the one they had courted on delivered to their new home to greet Marie on their return.

But imagine their shock when they returned to find not one, but two park benches sitting in their foyer. It seems that Marie had had the same idea.

The park benches, always proudly occupying a place of honor, have adorned three houses and twelve years of their lives.

Their sentimental gesture is unique, but most of us, if we think about it, have certain possessions that have special meaning for us. These are things we should always keep close.

I've always known my husband was more sentimental than I, but I realized how sentimental he was when, six years after we married, he confessed that he could not bear to throw away a checked wool jacket that he had worn on our honeymoon. He also stopped me from throwing away a ragged flannel nightgown he had given me one winter when he had whisked me away to a ski house in Vermont.

I decided I had to do something with these items, or we would soon have a closet full of clothes we no longer wore but couldn't bear to part with. I bought complementary material for each garment, and had them made into patchwork pillows. The pillows go on our bed every day. This way, our mementos don't lie unseen in a drawer but are part of our daily lives.

Look around and see what you can do to incorporate your most sentimental belongings into your real life.

## Marry Me, Marry Me

When Oliver, never one for the small gesture when he could arrange a big one, decided to propose to my friend Samantha, he didn't go down on his knees and present her with a small black velvet box. Instead he purchased a billboard along the road that Samantha drove to work on every morning and adorned it with this message: "Marry me, Samantha. I love you. Oliver."

## Very Special Delivery

Astronaut Millie Hughes-Fulford and her husband and daughter work on their grand gesture year-round. They are known for their special and very personal Christmas baskets.

Their farm, where they keep bees and maintain an orchard, is their base of operations. They gather honey and store it in pretty jars. When their apricot trees yield fruit, they gather that and make their own special apricot jam.

All year long, they scout antique and flea markets for charming baskets and old napkins. At Christmas, they put everything together—the baskets are lined with the pretty napkins, and a jar of honey and a jar of jam, along with a box of croissants, are added. Much of their fun is choosing who will get which basket, but the most fun is watching people's faces when they deliver their gifts in person.

## Pearls and Champagne

For their fifth wedding anniversary, Tom arranged for him and his wife to have dinner with friends. She assumed they would exchange presents later, when they were alone. So she was especially amazed to find a strand of stunning pearls draped across her champagne glass.

# You're My Cup of Tea

Like most of us, Shelley had fond memories of a favorite childhood possession. She had shared with her husband, Martin, the memory of a cup and saucer whose charm was enhanced, no doubt, by the fact that it was made by a china manufacturer who shared her name. Her cup and saucer had been lost, however. She had never seen another until last year when she found one on her vacation, in an antiques store in Georgia. The price tag put her off, however, and even though Martin urged her to buy it, she refused.

Two months later, on her birthday, Shelley opened her present from Martin and was amazed to find not the cup she had wanted but another Shelley china cup and saucer. She began to suspect she was in the middle of a grand gesture when she learned how her husband had gotten the cup.

After they had returned home, Martin called the antiques shop to order the cup, but the owner flatly refused to ship such a small item despite Martin's offer to pay mailing costs. An inventive, persistent man, Martin next called a friend who frequented flea markets and asked him to be on the lookout for Shelley cups and saucers. The friend found one for Shelley's birthday.

If Shelley suspected she was in the middle of a grand gesture, she knew she was when other cups and saucers began showing up on other gift-giving occasions. She soon learned that Martin had placed a standing order with his friend to buy any Shelley cups and saucers he found.

## A Gift of Love—and Leaving

As I've observed before, the best gifts are often about time—not only knowing when to show up for a loved one, but also knowing when to depart. Michele McCormick, whose father, Jack Watson, was my great friend until he died last year, wrote a memorial article about her father this past Father's Day. In it she recounted the many joys of their wonderful relationship, but one incident stands out in particular.

Imbued with her father's incurable sense of wanderlust, Michele had planned to take off for a season of meditation on the Spanish island of Mallorca after college. Her seemingly directionless life led her parents to question her goals, but they didn't forbid her to go.

One evening the telephone rang in her hotel room. It was Jack, who asked her how she was and listened while she rambled on about her self-described "transcendental revelations."

Suddenly she observed, "This connection is really good. It sounds like you're right here."

"I am," he said. He was calling from the lobby of her hotel. Jack hung out with Michele long enough to satisfy his curiosity that she was okay, and then left her, heading off on his own to explore Algeria.

*Showing Love*
*Throughout the Year*

# Wedding Anniversaries

| | |
|---|---|
| First | Paper |
| Second | Cotton |
| Third | Leather |
| Fourth | Silk |
| Fifth | Wood |
| Sixth | Iron |
| Seventh | Wool, copper |
| Eighth | Bronze |
| Ninth | Pottery |
| Tenth | Tin, aluminum |
| Eleventh | Steel |
| Twelfth | Linen (for bed or table) |
| Thirteenth | Lace |
| Fourteenth | Ivory |

| | |
|---|---|
| Fifteenth | Crystal |
| Twentieth | China |
| Twenty-fifth | Silver |
| Thirtieth | Pearl |
| Thirty-fifth | Jade, coral |
| Fortieth | Ruby |
| Forty-fifth | Sapphire |
| Fiftieth | Gold |
| Fifty-fifth | Emerald |
| Sixtieth | Diamond |
| Seventy-fifth | Diamond—again |

# Birthstones and Flowers

| January | Garnet | Snowdrop |
| March | Amethyst | Primrose |
| March | Aquamarine, bloodstone, jasper | Violet |
| April | Diamond | Daisy |
| May | Emerald | Hawthorn |
| June | Pearl, moonstone | Rose |
| July | Ruby | Water lily |
| August | Sardonyx, peridot, carnelian | Poppy |
| September | Sapphire | Morning glory |
| October | Opal | Water lily |
| November | Topaz | Chrysanthemum |
| December | Turquoise, lapis lazuli | Holly |

# Holidays Around the World

Every day can be cause for celebration with your loved ones. Here are some holidays around the world plus some quirky, loving, offbeat events you may never have thought to celebrate before.

## January

| | |
|---|---|
| 1 | New Year's Day; Liberation Day, Cuba |
| 2 | Berchtoldstag, Switzerland; Kakizome, Japan (traditional festival where the first strokes of the year are made on paper with special brushes) |
| 3 | Genshi-Sai (First Beginning) in Japan |
| 5 | Twelfth Night, end of medieval Christmas festivities, night of merriment |

| | |
|---|---|
| 6 | Epiphany, Catholic countries in Europe and Latin America<br>La Befana, Italy, an Epiphany feast (Befana, a witch, gives children toys and candy if they've been good, a lump of coal if they've been bad. The night before is cause for noisemaking and merriment) |
| 15 | Martin Luther King, Jr. Day; Adults' Day, Japan |
| 22 | Saint Vincent's Feast Day, Europe (patron saint of wine growers is feted; if sun shines, wine crop will be good) |
| Fourth Tuesday in January | Clash Day, wear mismatched outfits |
| 26 | Republic Day, India |
| 29 | Australia Day |

| | |
|---|---|
| January–February | Chinese New Year and Vietnamese New Year (Tet) |

**February**

| | |
|---|---|
| 2 | Groundhog Day; día de la Candelaria, Mexico (dances and parades); Candlemas, Europe (children serenade neighbors and are given sweets in return) |
| 3 | Setsubun, Japan (bean-throwing festival) |
| First Sunday in February | Hamstrom, Switzerland straw men are burned on poles to celebrate the imminent departure of winter |
| 14 | Valentine's Day, USA |
| 22 | Washington's Birthday, USA |
| 26 | Grand Canyon's birthday, USA |

| 27 | Independence Day, Dominican Republic |

| Late February–early March | Purim, Jewish (children's holiday) |

## March

| 8 | Women's Independence Day, many countries |

| 10 | Telephone invented, as in "Mr. Watson, come here, I want to see you" —1876 |

| 17 | St. Patrick's Day, Ireland and USA |

| 21 | Benito Juárez's birthday, Mexico |

| 22 | National Goof-Off Day. Go for it. |

| 23 | Near-Miss Day, recalls day in 1989 when mountain-size asteroid passed within 500,000 miles of Earth. Whew. |

| 25 | Independence Day, Greece |
| Late March–early April | Passover, Jewish |
| March–April | Carnival; Lent; Easter |

**April**

| 1 | April Fool's Day; Victory Day, Spain |
| 8 | Hana-matsuri (Buddha's Birthday), Korea, Japan; (Flower Festival) |
| 14 | Pan American Day |
| 22 | Earth Day (to honor our planet); Queen Isabella Day, Spain. |
| 25 | Liberation Day, Italy |
| 27 | Quadlings of Oz Day (celebrating Dorothy's meeting with Glinda, the good witch who told her about the magic shoes that would take her back to Kansas) |

| 28 | Kiss-Your-Mate Day. You know what to do with this one. |
| 30 | Queen's Birthday, The Netherlands |

## May

| 1 | May Day (ancient holiday celebrating arrival of spring in Western world and marked by maypoles, dancing, and workers' demonstrations in USSR, Europe, and Latin America); Lei Day in Hawaii (give them, wear them, display them) |
| 5 | Children's Day, Japan, Korea; Liberation Day, The Netherlands |
| Second Sunday in May | Mother's Day, USA |
| Third Sunday in May | Armed Forces Day, USA |
| 12 | Limerick Day. Write one . . . or two. |

| | |
|---|---|
| 20 | Eliza Doolittle Day (emphasizes importance of speaking one's native language properly) |
| First Monday before May 25 | Victoria Day, Canada |
| 30 | Memorial Day, USA |

**June**

| | |
|---|---|
| 10 | Portugal Day |
| 14 | Flag Day, USA |
| Third Sunday in June | Father's Day |
| Mid-June | Queen's Birthday, Great Britain |
| 17 | German Unity Day, Germany |
| 22 | Midsummer's Day, Finland |
| 24 | Midsummer's Day, Great Britain |

| 27 | "Happy Birthday to You" (day the song was composed by Mildred J. Hill, schoolteacher) |

| 29 | Feast of Saints Peter and Paul, Italy, Spain, Chile, Venezuela, Peru, and Colombia |

## July

| 1 | Canada Day, Canada; Half Year Holiday, Hong Kong |

| 2 | Thurgood Marshall's Birthday |

| 4 | Independence Day, USA |

| 5 | Independence Day, Venezuela |

| 9 | Independence Day, Argentina |

| 10 | Bon (Feast of Fortune), Japan |

| 11 | National Cheer-Up-the-Lonely Day |
| 14 | Bastille Day, France |
| 18 | National Day, Spain |
| 21–22 | National Holiday, Belgium |
| 22 | National Liberation Day, Poland |

## August

| 1 | Lammas Day, Great Britain; National Day, Switzerland |
| First Sunday in August | Friendship Day |
| 12 | Queen's Birthday, Thailand |
| 15 | Independence Day, India, Korea |

## September

| | |
|---|---|
| All month | Rose of Tralee Festival, Ireland |
| First Monday in September | Labor Day, USA, Canada |
| 7 | Independence Day, Brazil |
| 9 | Choxo-no-Sekku (Chrysanthemum Day), Japan |
| 10 | Swap Ideas Day (ideas to improve the world, that is) |
| 15 | Respect for Aged Day, Japan; Independence Day, Costa Rica, Nicaragua, Guatemala |
| 16 | Independence Day, Mexico |
| Mid-September | Sherry Wine Harvest, Spain |
| Late September–early October | Rosh Hashanah, Jewish New Year (culminates in Yom Kippur, Day of Atonement) |

## October

| | |
|---|---|
| 4 | Confucius's Birthday, Hong Kong, Taiwan |
| Second Monday in October | Thanksgiving, Canada |
| 6 | Erntedank Festival (Potato Festival), Germany |
| First Sunday in October | Grandparents' Day |
| 7 | Universal Children's Day, United Nations |
| 9 | Korean Alphabet Day, Korea |
| 10 | Giuseppe Verdi's Birthday (Celebrate all opera!) |
| 12 | Columbus Day, USA, Spain, Latin America |
| 13 | Interplanetary Confederation Day. Awareness of other planets in Milky Way |

| | |
|---|---|
| 19 | Sweetest Day (Okay, so go buy candy again.) |
| 26 | National Holiday, Austria |
| 28 | Greek National Day, Greece |
| 31 | Halloween |

## November

| | |
|---|---|
| 1 | All Saints' Day, most Catholic countries |
| 2 | All Souls' Day, Latin America, Luxembourg; Sadie Hawkins Day, USA (women ask men out, commemorated since 1930s in L'il Abner comic strip) |
| 3 | Sandwich Day (birthday of John Montague, Fourth Earl of Sandwich, and inventor of same) |
| 4 | National Unity Day, Italy |

| | |
|---|---|
| 5 | Guy Fawkes Day, Great Britain |
| 7–8 | October Revolution Day, USSR |
| 11 | Veterans' Day, USA, Belgium, France; Remembrance Day, Canada |
| 12 | Sun Yat-sen's Birthday, Taiwan |
| 17 | Federal Day of Penance, Germany |
| 19 | National Holiday, Monaco |
| Fourth Thursday in November | Thanksgiving, USA |
| 23 | Labor Thanksgiving Day, Japan |
| Fourth Friday in September | American Indian Day |

## December

| | |
|---|---|
| 6 | Independence Day, Finland |
| 10 | Human Rights Day, United Nations |
| 12 | Guadalupe Day, Mexico |
| Mid-December | Nine Days of Posada, Mexico |
| 25 | Christmas Day, Christian countries |
| 26 | Boxing Day, Canada, Great Britain (day when boxed gifts were expected by postman, lamplighter, dustman) |
| | Blessing of the Wine, Luxembourg |
| | Saint Stephen's Day, Austria, Ireland, Italy, Liechtenstein, Switzerland |

| | |
|---|---|
| 26–1/1 | Kwanzaa (African-American holiday since 1969 commemorating African harvest festivals) |
| Mid to late December | Chanukah (Jewish Festival of Light) |
| 31 | New Year's Eve, throughout world; Omisoka (Grand Last Day), Japan; Hogmanay Day, Scotland |

A Word to My Readers

Some of the gestures in this book are ones I've collected from my years of experience as an etiquette expert, but others are true-life examples that people have passed along to me. If you have a special way of showing love to someone in your life, and you'd like to share it with others, please write me:

Marjabelle Young Stewart
c/o St. Martin's Press, Inc.
175 Fifth Avenue
New York, NY 10010